Cropping Scrapbooks

Sarah McKenna

SEARCH PRESS

First published in Great Britain 2005

Search Press Limited
Wellwood, North Farm Road,
Tunbridge Wells, Kent TN2 3DR

Text copyright © Sarah McKenna 2005

Photographs by Roddy Paine Photographic Studios
Photographs and design copyright © Search Press Ltd 2005

ISBN 1 84448 076 3

The Publishers and author can accept no responsibility for any
consequences arising from the information, advice or
instructions given in this publication.

Readers are permitted to reproduce any of the items/patterns
in this book for their personal use, or for the purposes of selling
for charity, free of charge and without the prior permission of
the Publishers. Any use of the items/patterns for commercial
purposes is not permitted without the prior permission of the
Publishers.

Suppliers
If you have difficulty in obtaining any of the materials and
equipment mentioned in this book, then please write to the
Publishers, at the address above, for a current list of stockists,
including firms who operate a mail-order service. This list also
details some of the fonts used in scrapbooking projects.

Publisher's note
All the step-by-step photographs in this book feature the
author, Sarah McKenna, demonstrating cropping for
scrapbooks. No models have been used.

Dedication
For Emma, Annie, Charlsie and Katie, my very
own supermodels – with thanks!

Acknowledgements
I would like to thank:

My husband, Martin, for his patience and
especially for his good judgment and
encouragement.

Victoria for introducing me to scrapbooking in
the first place and for her enthusiasm, extra
photographs of various members of her family
and her many appearances in my own
photographs.

Susie and Roger for their excellent hospitality
during the production process and the
photographs of their lovely granddaughters.

My photography friends, Vicky, Geoff, Simon
and Steve, for their encouragement and extra
photographs.

Joy and Joanne at Cotswold Keepsakes for
their support and products.

The Scrapbook House and Eyelet Outlet
for products.

Roz, Felicity, Juan and Sophie at Search Press
for their help and guidance and Roddy Paine
for his perseverence on photography day.

Cover
Skiing in Zermatt
See page 21.

Page 1
Weston-super-Mare
I printed the saying round the edge on the background cardstock
by running the card four times through an A3 size printer. The
photographs were triple mounted on the finished page.

Opposite
Beach Babes
Here the torn edge of the photograph emphasises the breaking
waves at the girls' feet.

Contents

Introduction

I have had a passion for photography ever since I was given a Box Brownie camera at the age of nine, but it was not until 1997 that a friend working in the States introduced me to scrapbooking. As soon as I realised the opportunities that scrapbooking provided for displaying photographs in an interesting and inventive way, as well as capturing the stories behind the pictures in writing, I was hooked!

Cropping is one of the basics of scrapbooking and I use it to enhance the photographs in my albums, either by cutting the photographs themselves or the card and paper around them. In this book, I will show you many different cropping techniques and suggest when they can be used to best effect. You will also discover how to add titles and journaling and how to create a variety of effects that add interest, definition and texture to your pages.

One of the great joys of scrapbooking is that there is no right or wrong way of doing it. I hope I can inspire you to experiment because scrapbooking is a very personal way of storing your memories. Try combining cropping techniques with other craft tools that you might already use such as punches, stickers, stamps and more. Above all, I hope you will be able to use the ideas in this book to create beautiful scrapbook pages that reflect you.

4

discover

LETTERS

KATIE

18 May 1998

Memories are the
flowers in the garden
of life...

TAKE TIME
EVERY DAY
TO
BE SILLY!

Materials

There are only a few basic materials needed for scrapbooking: an album, cardstock to fit your album (the standard size is 30.5 x 30.5cm (12 x 12in) square), adhesive to fix the photographs and a pen or computer for adding text (this is known as journaling). Although these are the essentials, there are many additional materials that you can use on your album pages. Pages can be as simple or as complicated as you like and the crossover with other crafts, such as card making, sewing, collage, painting and rubber stamping, is enormous. It is essential that the paper, card and adhesive that touch your photographs are acid free so that your photographs are not damaged. Paper should also be lignin free otherwise it will deteriorate. I recommend that you buy material from reliable scrapbooking sources and look for labels which indicate that they are archival quality, photo-safe or acid free.

A guillotine and a smaller paper trimmer

Basic equipment

A **guillotine** capable of cutting 30.5 x 30.5cm (12 x 12in) cardstock is the best way to cut card and paper neatly and quickly. A **trimmer** or small guillotine is useful for smaller pieces of card and for photographs. **Scissors** are essential. I use a very small sharp pair for close cropping work, such as silhouetting.
Fancy-edged scissors are also available.
A **cutting mat** is necessary for use with a craft knife and other cutting tools. My cutting mat is self-healing and 33cm (13in) square which means I can work on a whole scrapbook page at once. It also has measurements marked on it, which is very useful. **Circle** and **oval cutters** come in a variety of designs which all work slightly differently. A **craft knife** allows you to cut accurately, for example, for hand-cut titles or where precise measurements are important, as with mosaics. I always use a cork-backed **metal ruler** as it works well with craft knives and does not slip. Unlike its acrylic counterpart, you cannot slice bits off it! **Craft punches** are used for punching out a variety of individual shapes from photographs, card or paper.
A **corner rounder** shapes the corners of card and photographs.

Clockwise from bottom right: fancy-edged scissors, small scissors, a craft knife, a corner rounder, craft punches in various sizes and designs, circle cutters, a cork-backed metal ruler and a self-healing cutting mat.

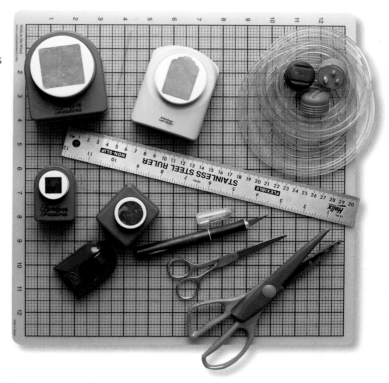

A **soft pencil, sharpener** and **eraser** will prove useful. A **photo-safe wax crayon** is helpful for marking cutting lines on photographs as it will not damage them and can be rubbed out later using a **photo-safe cloth**. Remove finger marks with **photograph cleaner**. **Gel pens** and **marker pens** are ideal for journaling and titles as long as they are acid free, fade resistant and waterproof. You can also create neat journaling with a more 'published' effect on a **computer**. Font packages are available on CD-ROM.

Adhesives come in many guises and you will probably need a variety of them for different purposes. **Photo tabs** and **double-sided tape** are useful for adhering cardstock, paper and photographs. **Glue pens** and **water-based adhesive** will fix light embellishments in place. Use **glue-dots** for attaching heavier bits and pieces. A regular **glue stick** is good for making items from cardstock, such as covering frames. **Repositionable tape** (available in a runner) is invaluable for temporarily attaching items while you consider your design. Finally, **adhesive remover** can be extremely useful if you need to take any part of your page apart!

Clockwise from bottom right: a soft pencil, photo-safe wax crayon, gel pens, marker pens, glue pen, water-based adhesive with nozzle, glue stick, repositionable tape in a tape runner, cleaning pad for use with photograph cleaner, photo-safe cloth, compact disc, large reel of double-sided tape, small reel of repositionable tape, box of photo tabs, glue dots in two different sizes, adhesive remover, photograph cleaner, eraser and pencil sharpener.

Paper and card

Most scrapbookers use standard cardstock squares to give a sturdy background to their layouts. Patterned or plain papers and various types of card are then added to create the page. Paper is available in a vast array of colours, textures and designs. What you choose will be determined by your own individual taste and the layout you are creating, but when you are selecting paper, ensure that it is acid and lignin free. Experiment with some of the lovely speciality papers available, such as vellum, textured paper or mesh, and use them to make interesting effects. However, your photographs are usually the focus of the page so keep to papers with subtle patterns and avoid designs that might be distracting, or use them sparingly. Acetate is useful for journaling and to create a layered look.

Cardstock, patterned paper, patterned vellum, plain paper, corrugated paper, embossed paper, plain vellum, mesh and acetate.

Albums

Albums come in a variety of sizes but the most popular in the UK is 30.5 x 30.5cm (12 x 12in). All of the layouts in this book were created on standard 30.5 x 30.5cm (12 x 12in) cardstock. Other sizes are available, for example 20.5 x 20.5cm (8 x 8in) and 15.5 x 15.5cm (6 x 6in), which make nice gift albums. Only use acid free albums. I find a top-loading album easiest to work with. The layouts are slipped into page protectors, which are then secured into the album on metal posts. This means that you can arrange the pages in any order, add extra pages if necessary and you do not have to work chronologically. Strap-bound albums, which have plastic straps to hook the pages on, are a popular alternative to top-loading albums.

A selection of 30.5 x 30.5cm (12 x 12in) and 20.5 x 20.5cm (8 x 8in) albums.

Embellishments

It is tempting to buy lots of the embellishments available but they are best used sparingly, otherwise they may overwhelm the page.

   Raffia, leather thread and **ribbons** or any attractive fibres are all great for attaching and threading **charms, buttons** and **beads** as well as being attractive in their own right. Beads can also be stuck directly on to your card using **strong double-sided tape.** Explore the haberdashery section at your local craft shop: **decorative rick-rack** might be just what you are looking for! **Twill tape** is made of fabric so you can stamp and paint on to it, or even print on it using a computer. **Tags** come in a range of different guises, including **metal-rimmed tags**, or you can make your own. **Wire** comes in a range of gauges and can be used in a similar way to raffia and ribbon. It is best cut with **wire cutters** to save damaging your scissors. **Metal book frames** are popular embellishments, as are **hinges** and **washers.** Paper fasteners such as **brads** and **safety pins** add interesting detail and also have a practical use in fixing photographs and other elements to your page. **Craft stickers** are available in a huge range of designs and materials, including fabric and 3D plastic. Do not neglect your own tickets, tokens, cards, leaflets, maps and other **memorabilia** as these details make your pages truly personal. It is best to spray them with **archival mist** before adhering them to your pages to ensure archival quality is preserved. Unusual **postage stamps** and **cigarette cards** are worth considering. **Rub-on transfers** come as sheets of letters or words. You position them and then rub the front of the transfer evenly with a blunt pencil or lolly stick (see page 45).

Clockwise from top: sticky-back fabric stickers, brads, butterfly charm, safety pins, metal bookplates and fastenings, shells, buttons, reels of coloured wire, wire cutters, beads, strong double-sided tape, roll of raffia, fibres, leather, white twill tape, floral rick-rack, ribbons, stamps, sheet of letter stickers, tile-effect 3D craft stickers, patterned acetate, tags, metal-rimmed tags and cigarette cards.

Other materials

You can borrow the techniques and materials of almost any craft that you enjoy when scrapbooking.

I frequently use **acrylic paints** for areas of background because they give me the freedom to mix exactly the colours I want. You could also use watercolours. **Textured paste** gives a three-dimensional aspect to your work. This thick paste looks like toothpaste when you apply it but dries hard. Some varieties of textured paste contain sand or gems, but once it is completely dry, you can also paint directly on to it. I use **brushes** and **rollers** of various sizes with paints and textured paste to achieve different effects (see pages 44–45).

Eyelets are embellishments but they are also ideal for fastening vellum, acetate and any thin material where glue might show through. An **eyelet tool kit** consists of a hole punch, a hammer, a setter and a setting mat. After punching a hole through your cardstock, you set the eyelet in the hole.

To create a rustic or aged look, rub **pigment ink** in inkpads, **chalks** or **rub-on paints** along the straight or torn edges of cardstock and photographs. Coloured chalk can be applied with a **cotton wool make-up pad** or small **chalk applicator** (see page 31). Rub-on paints come in ready-made palettes and have the consistency of lipstick. You apply them, as the name suggests, by rubbing them on with your finger.

Rubber stamps are available in many designs and can be used to make wonderful effects with water-based paint, pigment ink or a **clear inkpad** and chalks. Applying more than one colour to a rubber stamp makes an interesting, mottled image (see the shell detail on page 35).

You can create stylish details with **embossing powder**, rubber stamps and a **heating tool**. The process is simple: press a rubber stamp into a clear inkpad, apply the stamp to your cardstock, shake embossing powder over the area and heat with the heating tool. The powder melts to give a raised, metallic finish in the shape of the rubber stamp (see page 31). I use **tweezers** to hold the card that I am embossing away from my fingers to avoid burning them!

There are many ways of creating lettering by hand (see pages 38–41), including using a **letter stencil** but you could invest in a **die cut machine** (right). A range of different fonts in many sizes and various dies are available for them.

Clockwise from top: a heating tool, clear inkpad, embossing powder, textured paste, plate, turquoise acrylic paint, white acrylic paint, paint brush, foam roller, sand, sandpaper, metallic rub-on paints, letter stencil, cotton wool make-up pad, chalks, small chalk applicator, eyelet tool kit and eyelets, tweezers, rubber stamps in different designs and pigment inkpads.

Basics

Photographs arranged on cardstock or paper and other card form the basis of an album page. Album pages are often referred to as 'layouts', particularly when the design spreads over two adjoining pages. Before you begin arranging photographs, card or paper on an album page, it is often necessary to cut the photographs to size in some way and this is known as 'cropping'.

Cropping has many advantages. You can focus attention on a certain part of the photograph by cutting out any distracting background. You can cut a photograph in any number of ways, and each one will create a completely different design. In a sense, it is 'photo art'. Sometimes, cropping simply allows you to fit more photographs on your page.

The market

I love the colour and vibrancy of the produce in foreign markets and wanted to create a layout that really emphasised this. The photographs for this page were cropped into 5 x 7.5cm (2 x 3in) rectangles using a trimmer.

Cutting

Craft knife

When you are using a craft knife, always cut on a cutting mat. To make straight, accurate lines, hold the edge of the blade against a cork-backed metal ruler. Press and angle the craft knife slightly towards the ruler when cutting.

Trimmer or guillotine

A trimmer is ideal for cutting small sections of photograph and card. Measurements marked on the trimmer make it easy to cut several pieces to the same size quickly. A larger guillotine is useful for cutting whole sheets of cardstock or larger photographs.

Scissors

A small pair of sharp scissors is invaluable for all close cropping work such as silhouetting (see page 36) and cutting out lettering (see page 38).

Paris

Here I have sliced a 30.5 x 20cm (12 x 8in) photograph in half, fixing each half to the top and bottom of the scrapbook page. I have then added a band of montage in the middle. The montage includes carefully cut photographs, journaling and memorabilia. This helps to give an impression of the holiday whilst stressing the monolithic structure that is the Eiffel Tower, which dominates the page just as it dominates the Paris skyline.

Circle cutters

You will be able to produce perfect circles if you invest in a set of circle cutters. These are cleverly designed so that you can combine the circles and blades in many different ways. For example, you can create a cardstock circle that is fractionally larger than your picture and this is ideal for creating a border (see 'Matting', page 12). Similar sets are also available in ovals.

1. Place the clear plastic circle over the relevant part of the photograph and position the cutting blade against it.

2. Drag the cutting blade all the way round the plastic circle. Then you can remove the cut-out circle.

Abigail and Sophie

Many of these photographs had distracting backgrounds. I cut them all into circles to focus attention on the children. Circles create a softer look than squares or rectangles. The montage in the middle follows the baby theme.

Matting

Matting your photographs is a basic scrapbooking technique. It involves sticking a photograph on to cardstock or paper and cutting round it to create a border. Matting enhances your photographs, adding interest and definition and creates a focal point on your page. There are various different methods of matting, depending upon the result you are trying to achieve. In this section I have explained some ideas that you will be able to adapt and use on your layouts.

1. Arrange three photographs on your backing card, allowing enough space between them to create a border. Keep any off-cuts of card for other projects.

2. When you are happy with the arrangement, remove one photograph at a time, attach photo tabs to the back and fix it in place on the backing card.

3. Line your card up on a guillotine so that the blade is parallel to the first photograph. Slice quickly and smoothly. When you reposition the mounted photograph to cut the next side, make sure that the space between the blade and the photograph is the same as it was before so that the border will be even. Repeat with your other photographs.

Tip
To get the cleanest cut from a guillotine, always pull the cutting blade slightly towards the guillotine itself as you cut downwards.

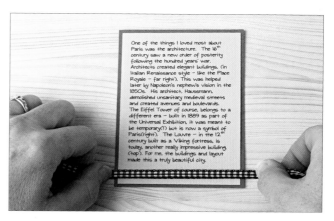

4. Double mount a fourth photograph using different coloured card. Now arrange all of your matted photographs on your page.

5. Write or type your chosen text neatly on to card and mat the card. Add a decorative detail such as ribbon. The ribbon pictured was fixed using repositionable tape.

Paris in the Springtime

The finished page. The mats around these pictures are quite narrow so that there is only a hint of colour. This looks more sophisticated than thick mats and keeps the focus on the photographs.

Matting a tag

Tags are available commercially but not necessarily in the size or colour that is right for your particular project. Making your own tag is the answer. This example uses a photograph but tags can feature journaling, stamping or any kind of embellishment.

1. To assess which area of the photograph you want to appear on your tag, hold it against a light with the back facing you. Roughly mark the edges of your tag shape using a photo-safe wax crayon.

2. Following your marks, cut away the long sides of the photograph. Draw a horizontal line 2.5cm (1in) down from the top and then two matching diagonal lines to create the tag shape.

3. Double mount the photograph and tear off, rather than cut, the bottom of the second piece of card.

4. Attach a sticker or a punched out shape to the top of the tag. Then, using an eyelet tool kit, hammer a hole through the sticker.

5. Thread attractive fibres through the hole.

Tip
Yellow is a very strong colour on layouts. I always work on the basis that a little bit of yellow goes a very long way!

Sharing a lilo!

Here is a photographic sequence of my daughter and me demonstrating how not to share a lilo! I have used turquoise and white to complement the pool water, with punched sun shapes providing splashes of yellow to give the impression of summer.

Matting a detail

This technique allows you to draw attention to a focal point in a photograph whilst preserving the background. I have used it here on an enlarged print but it works on smaller photographs, too.

1. Use repositionable tape to stick your photograph to the cutting mat. Draw a square around your chosen detail using a photo-safe wax crayon. Use a craft knife and metal ruler to cut it out.

2. Mat the cut-out detail and then position it back in its original place. Attach the matted detail using photo tabs.

Winter

Living in the middle of rural Gloucestershire can have its advantages. When it snows heavily, our lovely scenery changes into a winter wonderland. On the day pictured here, the roads and schools were closed so we set off to a friend's farm in the next valley to go sledging. For this layout, I wanted to highlight our little troop walking through the magical landscape. For me, the pictures say it all. A happy day indeed!

Composing a page

The very first thing I do before cutting any photographs or even choosing colours and card, is decide what type of page or layout I am trying to create. For example, am I trying to display a single photograph or perhaps a number of photographs of an occasion over a two-page layout? This will determine the size of the layout.

Mood

Next, I decide what mood I am trying to capture. So, my second question when planning a page or layout is, 'What is the main message I want to convey?' It might be happy, serious, fun, active or contemplative. The mood of the photograph should be your starting point and it will affect your choice of colours, textures and embellishments. I have created pages for four very different photographs to illustrate this point.

Tip
I rarely crop heritage photographs. Their original style usually adds to the aged theme.

Wedding

This black and white photograph has a nostalgic, romantic feel so I have chosen softly patterned papers and vellum, tearing the edges to make them softer still. Silver edging on the vellum and tag, foil embellishments and some silver embossing add to the sense of celebration. Gold would also work well with the wedding theme but I prefer silver with black and white photographs. Although you can put virtually any colour with black and white photographs, I have used a deep, cranberry-coloured background. For me, this helps to focus on the serious side of a wedding. Bright red or turquoise would have gone with the photograph but would not have conveyed the right mood at all.

Sassy

This photograph of my daughter Emma is really punchy; it jumps off the page. It was important not to drown it in detail but to keep the uncomplicated, striking look. I have chosen simple but vividly coloured lines and a hand-cut title in a contemporary font style. The colours, including the black background, add to the modern feel. The red picks up the red in the photograph and lime green adds just a touch of interest without being overwhelming. Note that the red photograph mat is very thin, which is part of the graphic style.

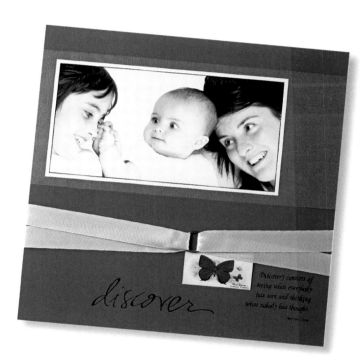

Family

This is a lovely, soft and feminine shot of mother, baby and older daughter. Traditionally, babies are associated with pastel colours but my personal preference is for colours with more depth. I have chosen relatively muted colours because I do not want to ruin the soft theme, but they are not as 'wishy-washy' as pastel shades. I want the photograph to be the focus so I have kept the embellishments very simple with the baby blue ribbon my sole concession to pastels!

Sisters

Although the pose in this photograph is quite static, the bright sunlight and Katie's jazzy top scream summer fun. When choosing paper for my pages, I often take photographs to the craft shop with me so that I can match colours and designs. I felt that I had to design the page around Katie's top and the photograph can take bright colours and boldly patterned paper. I was lucky, the paper manufacturer might almost have modelled the design of the paper on Katie's summer vest! For the mat, I used brown cardstock and softened it using a mixture of white and a little brown acrylic paint applied with a roller (see page 44). This softens the brown and brings in the texture of the wall in the photograph. The girls chose the quotation for the page themselves.

Atmosphere

The key to creating atmosphere is choosing the right colours, techniques, texture of paper and embellishments to suit your photographs. For example, if you have a layout set in an historic city, you might choose colours that harmonise with the stonework. If you want to emphasise the formality of the buildings, you might arrange the photographs straight rather than at an angle. You can then add carefully chosen embellishments which have the look of that historical period (see pages 42–43, 'Venice'). If, on the other hand, you have a picture of a modern cityscape, you might choose metallic papers or use layers of acetate. Embellishments in this case would be simple and bold. If a day on a farm is your theme, corrugated paper or suede combined with gingham, raffia or string will give a rustic feel. Torn edges and chalking or inking could also work well.

Outdoor fun

The children were in their element when we went to this water park in France for the day. A bright turquoise background unifies the layout because turquoise appears in all the photographs. The shade that I have chosen complements the colour of the water and water slides. As I wanted to include a lot of photographs, I limited the use of patterned paper to avoid making the layout too busy. The paper I used has a 'watery' feel. This layout is all about enjoyment and activity, so cutting the photographs into different shapes and arranging them at angles adds to the overall sense of vitality. All the embellishments are in keeping with the watery theme.

Stormy weather

These photographs were taken off the coast of Norway in a stormy week. I picked sombre colours to help to emphasise the stormy conditions, with just a hint of mustard yellow for the journaling. The yellow brings out the colours in the rainbow. I placed the photographs at an angle to give the impression that all is not calm! Two small matted maps cut from the holiday brochure locate the storm. I created the title using rub-on transfers which, being slightly textured and rough, add to the idea of rough seas. The gingham ribbon that forms a frame was lightly rubbed with an inkpad before it was attached. This helps to add to the stormy atmosphere.

Emphasis

There are many cropping techniques that you can use to emphasise certain aspects of your photographs. The shapes you crop, the embellishments you add, even the arrangement of your pictures together contribute to the overall 'message' of the page.

Use a corner punch to create bricks from rectangles of paper in shades of brown.

Hadrian's Wall

This is a simple page using some old walking photographs. To emphasise the idea of the wall, I have built one from cardstock scraps!

A pair of fancy-edged scissors will give your matting interesting and unusual edges. They are available in many different designs.

Tree climbing

At my in-laws' house there was an old tree that the children used to enjoy climbing. I have turned the photographs of them doing this into a tree shape by cutting them into circles of different sizes, matting them on green cardstock and creating interesting edges using fancy-edged scissors.

Skiing in Zermatt

Six diamond shapes together make a snowflake, which is very appropriate for photographs of skiing. This is also a good way of fitting several photographs on a page.

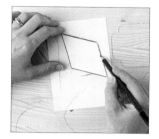

I held each photograph and a stencil up to the light to mark out the shape (see page 14). I then cut out each diamond with a craft knife and metal ruler.

Play

The motion of the swing is emphasised by the wavy edge that I cut into the pale green cardstock. Placing the photographs and the title at an angle also contributes to the sense of movement. I used a mixture of white, green and brown acrylic paint applied with a roller on the background cardstock. Using the same paint mix, I placed the cut letters on a rough piece of cardstock and simply rolled the paint over them. After they had dried, I stuck them to the layout.

Norfolk

Use your imagination when adding emphasis. Here the children wrote the title on the beach with stones, which I then photographed! The strips of mosaic at the top and bottom of this page capture aspects of our Norfolk holiday.

Playfulness

Robert enjoyed peering through the yellow rings in the play area. The layout emphasises this by replicating the rings. Although the photograph was taken on a dull day, the page colours help to 'lift' it – red to match Robert's trousers, yellow for the rings and green to tie in with the background. Using blocks of colour is an easy way to create a unified layout.

ROBERT MICHAEL
NOYES
May 1996

Robert was so deeply unimpressed with the day's activities that, as if in protest, he refused to eat anything other than chocolate digestive biscuits.

This was Brownie Sports Day. Robert, aged 2 and a half, was none too impressed with being left with his Aunt and a bevy of girls for the day. He wandered off to play on something that interested him with a mischievous look in his eyes.

Katie & Martin
Provence
August 2004

A daughter may outgrow your lap ....
but she will never outgrow your heart

Katie and Martin

Here I focused on Katie's round earrings and skirt which are both black polka dot. I cut a large circle from the background tan cardstock and placed polka dot paper behind. Note that inking the edges of the cardstock titles helps them to stand out. This technique is demonstrated on page 30.

Plum picking

I have enlarged a photograph of plum trees and used that as a frame for the images of pigs in an orchard. A rustic feel is created by choosing a textured card for the background, using rub-on paint along its edges and framing the title in brown cardstock.

Painting & decorating

The pale pink cardstock has been distressed using sandpaper, an effect that links the background to the photographs and to the overall theme of decorating a bedroom. The photographs have also been sanded and the title was painted on using foam stamps, as if with emulsion.

23

Techniques

The wonderful thing about scrapbooking is that you can use a limitless range of techniques on your pages. All you need to keep in mind is the message you are trying to convey, but beyond that there are no rules! I never cease to be amazed at how unique and individual each scrapbooker's style is.

Frames: Views of Bath

The right frame will make your photograph stand out on the page. If your design contains more than one photograph, framing will create a focal point. The type of frame you use will contribute to the overall mood of the page. For example, 'Annie the Bridesmaid' (see page 27) has a formal look while James jumping through a triangular frame (see page 29) is fresh and active.

This frame is easy to make and can be adapted to suit many projects. Simply change the proportions of the frame and experiment with different ways of decorating the card that you have used.

You will need

Photographs

Dark green cardstock,
30.5 x 30.5cm (12 x 12in)

Two sheets of apple-green cardstock,
30.5 x 30.5cm (12 x 12in)

Patterned paper,
30.5 x 30.5cm (12 x 12in)

Sheet of vellum

Craft knife and cutting mat

Metal ruler

Photo tabs

Double-sided tape

Hole punch

Rubber stamp and gold inkpad

Green brad

Ribbon

Eight green eyelets and eyelet tool kit

Lime green acrylic paint

Paper piercer

Sticker machine (optional)

Pen or computer

1. Measure out four rectangles for your frame on cardstock and cut them out. Make sure that they are long enough to overlap each other at the corners.

2. Cut the corners off the top and bottom of the two short sections of the frame. Line up each end with the grid on your cutting mat and slice the corner off diagonally.

3. Use photo tabs to attach the short sections of the frame to the long sections. Place the frame on a piece of scrap paper and stamp all over it using a rubber stamp. Stamp over the edges as shown.

4. Use double-sided tape to fix your photograph to the back of the frame. Use the hole punch from the eyelet tool kit to make two holes at the top and thread ribbon through. To attach your frame to the page, make a hole using a paper piercer as shown.

5. Attach a brad and tie the ends of the ribbon around it. Use photo tabs to stick your frame in the desired position on the page.

The finished layout. I built it up using more photographs and patterned paper. For the title, 'Bath', I used lime green acrylic paint on vellum and it over a photograph using eyelets. The journaling and smaller titles were created on the computer, then stuck over green card using a sticker machine.

Frames 2: Annie the Bridesmaid

This frame is simple to make but gives a sophisticated finish. Essentially it is a covered frame. Once you have mastered the technique, you can make similar frames of any size and cover them in whatever paper suits your page.

You will need

Photograph

Cream cardstock,
30.5 x 30.5cm (12 x 12in)

Cardstock for the frame,
30.5 x 30.5cm (12 x 12in)

Vellum,
30.5 x 30.5cm (12 x 12in)

Patterned paper,
30.5 x 30.5cm (12 x 12in)

Ribbon

Tiny white tag

Marker pen

Metallic rub-on paints

White rub-on transfers

Metal bookplate

Five small metallic brads

Glue stick

Metal ruler

Craft knife and cutting mat

Photo tabs

Pencil

Pen or computer

Paper piercer

Leaf skeletons

1. First measure your photograph to determine the size of the frame. The inside of the frame needs to be slightly smaller than the photograph you are framing. Use a pencil and ruler to measure out your complete frame on a piece of cardstock.

2. Cut the frame out using a craft knife and metal ruler.

3. Place your patterned paper face down on a cutting mat. Use glue stick to glue the frame to the paper. Now cut around the frame leaving a margin that is slightly less than the width of the frame.

4. Cut around the inside of the frame leaving a smaller margin and remove the paper rectangle that cutting creates. Now cut off each corner at a diagonal, leaving a small space between the frame and the cut, as shown.

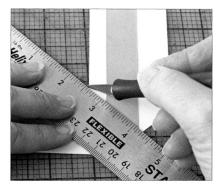 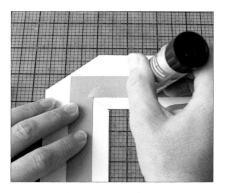 

5. Cut a diagonal line at each corner on the inside of the frame, taking care not to cut through the frame.

6. Spread glue over the frame. This gives a neater result than trying to put glue on the paper.

7. Fold over the inner paper edges first, then the outer paper edges. Smooth them all down. Attach the frame to your photograph using photo tabs and build your scrapbooking page. To attach a sheet of vellum, make holes with a paper piercer (see page 25) and then add the brads. Embellish the page using text, a metal bookplate, ribbon, rub-on transfers and a tag.

The finished layout. I added a tiny tag with the words 'Aged 4' and gave it a vintage feel using rub-on metallic paints. Rub-on transfers were used to create the word 'dream'. The journaling was typed on a computer, and leaf skeletons were added for a delicate touch.

I love this very wistful photograph of Annie. I framed it to enhance the feeling of her looking out of the church door and used pale, softly coloured paper and vellum for a romantic look.

(Page based on an idea by Karen McIvor of Scrapaholic Ltd)

Framing a detail

Framing a detail within the photograph rather than the picture itself is striking and unusual.

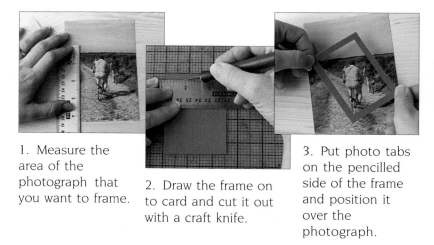

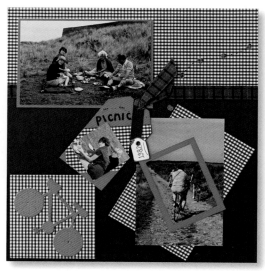

1. Measure the area of the photograph that you want to frame.

2. Draw the frame on to card and cut it out with a craft knife.

3. Put photo tabs on the pencilled side of the frame and position it over the photograph.

Picnic

Making a negative frame

Decide where to position your frame on the page before you start drawing and cutting. Remember that if you draw your frame on the right-hand side of the page, when you turn it over it will appear on the left-hand side.

1. Measure your picture. Then draw three rectangles as shown, the smallest of which must be slightly smaller than your photograph.

2. Use a craft knife and metal ruler to cut round your rectangles. Discard the larger frame, fix decorative paper under the 'hole' and fix the picture and smaller frame in place using photo tabs.

Sisters

Fixing a frame with eyelets, snaps or brads

This frame is simplicity itself: four strips of card fixed in place with either eyelets, snaps or brads. It looks casual here with overlapping edges, but if each strip was lined up straight, it would look more formal.

1. Cut out two long and two short strips of card. Arrange them in the shape of a frame over the photograph on your page. I have also placed mesh underneath the photograph here.

2. Fix the photograph to the mesh using photo tabs. Now hammer in a snap at each corner using tools from your eyelet kit.

Eyes

Making a triangular frame

A triangular frame emphasises action. Measure your photograph first as your frame needs to be as big as, or slightly bigger than, the picture.

1. Draw a diagonal line down the length of your cardstock.

2. Position a protractor at the end of the line and mark a 60° angle.

3. Draw in the second line at a 60° angle, then complete the triangle. Draw a smaller triangle inside this one, according to the size of frame you need. Cut out the frame with a craft knife and slip it over the picture.

James

Effects

There are all kinds of exciting visual effects that you can use on your projects.
Again, the trick is to pick effects that are appropriate for the scrapbook page
in question.

Double-sided tape and beads

Beads are available in all the colours of the rainbow and if you match them well
to your theme, they can add a fun twist to your page. Clear or blue/green beads
are ideal for seaside or poolside pictures.

1. Place double-sided tape in the area where you want beads. Peel off the backing.

2. Simply shake beads evenly over the double-sided tape. Shake off the excess.

Take time every day to be silly

Inking and sanding

You can ink the edges of photographs, mats or entire pieces of cardstock.
Inking adds dimension to the page and can produce an aged look.
Sanding also ages paper, tones down strong patterns and creates texture.

Pull an inkpad along the edge of your card or paper. Inking the card in this way adds subtle definition to the edges.

Gently remove the surface of patterned paper using grade three sandpaper.

Belton House

Tearing and chalking

Tearing paper or photographs creates a rough edge which can then be chalked to blend in with your page. This works well with seaside and snow scenes.

1. Tear the edge of the photograph slowly towards you.

2. Use a cotton wool pad to rub a little chalk in to the torn edge.

Glue and thread

Thread adds interest and texture. Here the threads mimic the rays of the sun and also cover each join where two pieces of different coloured card meet.

1. Use a fine-tip glue applicator to add a line of glue along the join.

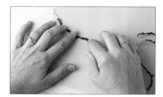

2. Press your decorative thread on to the glue.

Embossing

Embossing adds a richness to your page that is perfect for a wedding theme but take care not to overdo it – it can be garish. The powder is available in a variety of thicknesses and colours.

1. Press the stamp into an embossing inkpad and stamp along the edge of your card.

2. Scatter embossing powder over the stamped area. Shake off the excess powder and return it to the pot.

3. Hold a heating tool over the stamped area and the powder will melt. Leave to cool.

WARNING Heating tools get extremely hot. Keep your hands away from the heat source. If in doubt, use tweezers to hold the card. Work on a heat-proof surface.

Summer in the South of France

Katie

The title was created on an ink-jet printer and embossed before the ink dried.

Annie snorkelling

This was Annie's first experience of flippers. They were far too big! I have enhanced the beach theme by adding sand and acrylic paint to the page. The title was made from stickers which were painted over and then removed. The technique is explained on page 36.

Family Malden

I have used traditional colours and an old-fashioned font style to enhance the heritage theme. Embossed paper seemed appropriate for the period feel and I used rub-on paints to age it. The names and dates on the strips identify the people in the picture and give the page a personal touch. The smallest boy on the table is my Dad! Note that the heritage photograph has not been cropped.

Me!

One method of adding extra texture is by crumpling the paper or card before you sand it. Here the red strips and mats have been crumpled into a ball, smoothed out and then sanded with grade three sandpaper. The background cardstock was also lightly sanded to make the overall look less formal. If you want to create an aged look, you can ink lightly over the sanded card with an inkpad. You can attach the crumpled card to your pages as it is or, if you want to make it flatter, iron the reverse of the cardstock using your iron's lowest setting.

(Page based on an idea by Karen McIvor of Scrapaholic Ltd. Photograph by Touch Studios)

Jump

I cut the photographs into arbitrary shapes and stuck the pieces on in a random arrangement at lots of different angles. This is a variation of the slicing technique shown on page 34. It gives an impression of movement. I embossed the background cardstock and the hand-cut title with snowflakes to underline the wintery theme.

Slicing: At the Seaside

Slicing is a technique that I use often. You cut two or more different photographs into segments and arrange the segments so that your pictures are interleaved. It is very simple technique but the results are dramatic. Before you begin, decide on the focal point of your picture and then slice off segments from either side. They can be cut evenly, unevenly or a mixture of both. You will find that slicing draws attention to the action in your photograph whilst giving your page an overall sense of liveliness and movement.

When my girls were little, we spent many summer holidays in Norfolk. For this project I wanted to create a visual representation of happy days on the beach. The 'touchy-feely' embellishments help the memory process, especially the shells which were collected at the time.

You will need

Photographs

Two sheets of pale blue cardstock, 30.5 x 30.5cm (12 x 12in)

Brown cardstock, 30.5 x 30.5cm (12 x 12in)

Cream cardstock for matting, 30.5 x 30.5cm (12 x 12in)

Two sheets of sand style patterned paper, 30.5 x 30.5cm (12 x 12in)

Craft knife and cutting mat

Trimmer

Double-sided tape

Photo tabs

Metal-rimmed tag

Shell rubber stamp and inkpad

Acetate

Computer or pen

'Summer' rub-on transfer

Fine string

Eight eyelets and eyelet tool kit

Four metallic brads

Sand, glue and foam roller

Netting

Shells

1. Select photographs that complement each other. In this case, three pictures of a similar view each taken at a different distance.

2. A trimmer or small guillotine will give you crisp, straight edges. Slice off segments at each side of the picture's focal point.

3. Reassemble your photographs on your work surface. This will make it easier to decide how best to interleave the segments.

4. Mat the segment featuring your focal point, then take time experimenting with the arrangement of your other segments on your work surface. Once you are completely happy with the design, fix them to your pages using photo tabs.

5. Build up your page using a range of effects and embellishments. Here I applied glue along the bottom of the page using a foam roller and sprinkled sand on it. I placed a stamped seashell stamp behind my journaling and added shells and netting. The netting is fixed to the back of the page using double-sided tape without removing the backing. The title is a rub-on transfer.

6. You can pick out a detail on your page using a frame made from a metal-rimmed tag. Using a craft knife, cut a cross into the tag as shown. Cut right the way up to each corner.

7. Push your finger through the middle of the cross and then carefully pull out each triangle of card. Glue the metal frame over your chosen detail.

8. A string frame is another way to add emphasis. Make four eyelet holes to thread the string through and stick each length at the back of the photograph as for the netting in step 5.

The finished layout. Interleaving segments of different photographs allows you to play with scale. For example, the groynes on the beach are exaggerated because they are cut from close-up photographs.

Silhouetting: The Sandcastle

Silhouetting means cutting away distracting backgrounds to leave your subject matter in silhouette, as the name suggests. It is an exceptionally useful technique. Along with removing unwanted areas of the picture, silhouetting also creates a slightly three-dimensional effect, creating album pages that really leap out at you. It is ideal for presenting a lot of photographs of one event, such as a party or gathering. Sometimes you are able to make an entirely new picture from your photographs using this technique.

Annie was very proud of her sandcastle! I wanted her sitting on the sandcastle to be the main focus of the picture. The two people standing directly behind her head were distracting, so I chose to silhouette the photograph.

You will need

Photographs
Turquoise cardstock,
30.5 x 30.5cm (12 x 12in)
Sand cardstock,
30.5 x 30.5cm (12 x 12in)
White acrylic paint
Paint brush
Letter stickers
Starfish rubber stamp
and inkpad
Dark-coloured inkpad
Photo tabs
Scissors
Glue stick
Tag craft punch
Hole punch
Raffia

1. Roughly tear the bottom off a piece of sand-coloured cardstock and stick it to your page using photo tabs. Add the title using letter stickers.

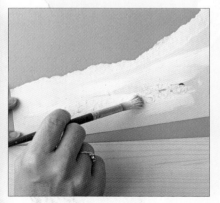

2. Loosely paint over the lettering with acrylic paint. Leave until nearly dry.

3. Carefully peel off each letter.

4. Cut closely around the edge of the detail that you wish to feature. Tuck the photograph under the sand-coloured card and then fix to the page using photo tabs.

5. Build up your page using another matted picture and effects such as stamping. In this case, a starfish is perfect for the theme.

6. Tags add interest to any page and here a tag draws attention to the top of the sandcastle. I printed the text on to card with the computer and then punched out the shape.

7. Use a hole punch to make a hole at the top of the tag and feed through a raffia tie. Ink the edges of the tag in a dark colour (see page 30) to give it extra definition.

Tip

Silhouetting seems simple but it is surprisingly easy to get it wrong. Two general points: always cut very close to the image when you are creating the silhouette. If you leave too much space around it, it will appear to float when you place it on the page. If you are silhouetting pictures of people, you will find that arms and legs often go out of frame in a photograph. Cover up these 'ends' with other elements on your page.

The finished page

Lettering

Recording memories is as much the purpose of scrapbooking as displaying photographs. Adding an eye-catching title and some journaling really helps to capture the feeling or moment that you want to record on your scrapbook page. Various methods of creating interesting letters and numbers for titles are described below. Hopefully you will be inspired to adapt the ideas to make numerous examples of your own!

Covering letters with collage

Collage works best with large letters as they give you the room to include lots of photographs. I tend to use them as the first letter in a title and complete the word with printed, painted or sticker letters.

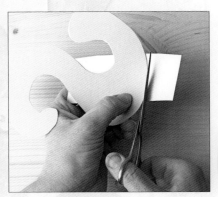

1. Draw a letter on to card and cut it out. Fix a small section of photograph to the letter using photo tabs.

2. Trim off the excess photograph, following the shape of the letter. Work your way around the letter adding and trimming different sections of photograph.

S for spring

You can trim around the shape of a detail in your picture, as I have here with the blossom, to give a layered effect.

Using stencils and stickers

Using one long sticker across the length of your title gives it impact and adds interest to your page.

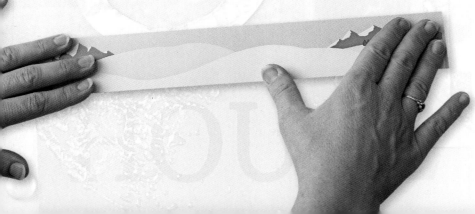

1. Stick a decorative sticker to a piece of card.

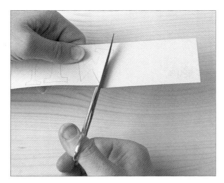

3. Carefully cut out each letter with a pair of sharp scissors.

2. Turn the piece of card over and, using a letter stencil face down, draw round the letters you require. Spell out the word from right to left.

Winter

When you turn each letter over you will find that the sticker has created an interesting pattern across the length of your word.

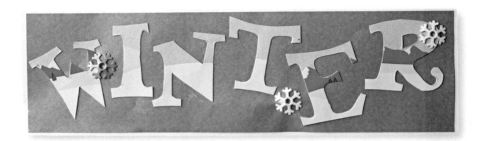

Shadow letters or numbers

This is another fun way to use a stencil but you need to cut neatly for this one!

1. Using the stencil face down, draw your letters or numbers on the back of a piece of gold paper. Use a craft knife to cut round each letter but do not pull them away from the paper. Instead, cut a line straight across the middle of the paper holding the cork-backed metal ruler down firmly.

2. Place the bottom section of gold paper on to cardstock and gently remove all parts of the numbers. Line up the top half of each number with the hole left by the bottom half. When you are happy with the positioning, fix with photo tabs.

2004

I used a star stamp and gold ink to create a subtle pattern on the background card. The title could be used for a New Year or Review of the Year page.

Cutting numbers or letters from a photograph

Before you begin, carefully consider where you are going to position your numbers or letters. Holding the photograph up to the light may help you decide (see page 14).

1. Put your stencil face down on the back of the photograph and draw round the relevant number with a pencil.

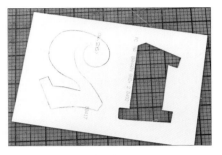

2. Use a craft knife to cut out the number on a cutting mat.

3. Mat your number and stick it back over the hole that it left in your photograph using photo tabs. Matting has two advantages; it adds definition and also covers up any evidence of cutting on the photograph itself.

Photo sandwich

Making a title with a photo sandwich using the same colour card as your background is a great way to co-ordinate your title with your page.

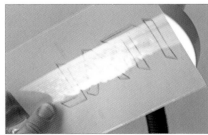

2. Turn the photograph over and stencil letters on the back, remembering to work from right to left. Holding the photograph up to the light will help you judge where to position the letters. Cut the letters out and remount them on your page.

1. Glue a strip of card across the top and bottom of a photograph but do not cover all of the picture. For added texture and interest one piece of card could be cut and the other torn.

I have used colours that complement the photograph, but you could use the colours of a country's flag.

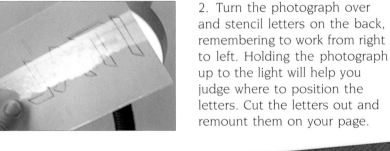

Using a detail from a photograph

This creative technique visually links the title to the photographs on the rest of the page. Some shapes lend themselves to certain letters: any tall structure or even a person can make an effective 'I'.

Cut out a detail that suggests a particular letter shape from a photograph. Build up the rest of the word using an alternative method of lettering.

Using computer fonts

Fonts can be printed straight on to card from a home computer and there is a vast and inspiring array of font styles available.

Select a font you like and adjust the size on screen. Use the 'rotate' and 'flip' functions to reverse your text (or refer to the instructions for reversing text with your software) and print it on to cardstock. Then cut each letter out by hand. This avoids the lines showing on the front.

Using a die cut machine

A die cut machine creates instant, professional-looking lettering. You can use the 'empty' negative cut letter shapes as well as the positive letters the machine stamps out as part of your page.

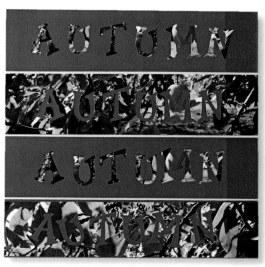

To cut out a letter, slip the card or photograph into the machine, place a letter block over it and under the handle barrier and press down hard.

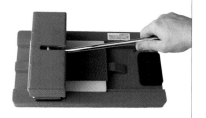

Decorative punching

If you are involved in other crafts such as card making, you may already have to hand many of the craft tools used in scrapbooking. Decorative craft punches are particularly versatile and useful to scrapbookers. A well-chosen punch can add the perfect touch to your page that will really bring out your theme. You can use the positive or negative image made by a punch and you may choose to punch through card, paper or even photographs.

Positive shapes

Punches are available in many designs so you should be able to find something appropriate to your theme. Simply place your card, paper or photograph in the punch and press down. Glue the resulting shape on to your work.

Negative shapes

You can also experiment with the negative shapes that punches leave behind. Try creating a decorative edge (see 'Forever'), or punching a row of the same design.

Impressions of Venice

In order to capture as many of the different scenes in this lovely city as possible, I decided to make a photographic mosaic (see pages 46–47). The design of the punch seems in keeping with Venetian architecture and mosaics are found all over the city. The two techniques combined contribute to the sense of place.

1. Turn a large square punch upside-down and place your photograph in it facing towards you. Position the detail in the square and push down hard to punch it out.

2. Use a small craft punch on paper matching your background cardstock.

3. Use a trimmer or guillotine to cut a square around your decorative punching. Then incorporate your punched pieces of card into the design.

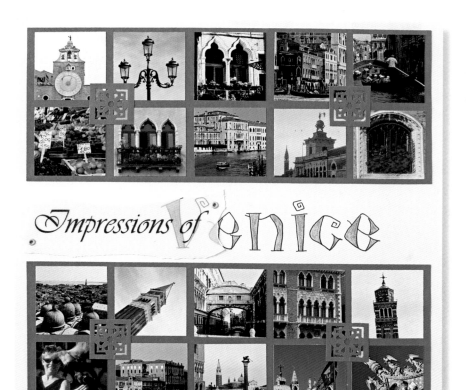

The finished layout. As well as focusing on details of the city, punched out photographs allow you to fit quite a number on a page, creating a vivid impression of the place.

Emma's bedroom

I have made a frame around two photographs of Emma's bedroom. The punched shapes stuck on to the frame help to emphasise that it is a child's bedroom.

Montage: Pool Matters

Montage is exciting because you can use any combination of cutting techniques to achieve the effect you want. The only limit is your imagination! It is a great means of fitting many different photographs on one page or layout, and the finished montage becomes a whole new picture in its own right.

I wanted this layout to celebrate happy days round a pool on a summer holiday. I had lots of photos to include so I cropped them to focus on the people. Cutting out circles adds to the theme of water and a random arrangement on the layout gives an active feel which complements the photographs. Note that I enlarged some of the photographs to give them extra punch.

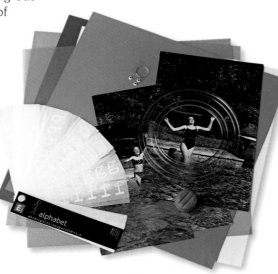

You will need

Two sheets of 30.5 x 30.5cm (12 x 12in) turquoise cardstock

Teal cardstock, 30.5 x 30.5cm (12 x 12in)

Turquoise vellum, 30.5 x 30.5cm (12 x 12in)

White cardstock, 30.5 x 30.5cm (12 x 12in)

Cutting mat

Scissors

Three white eyelets

Eyelet tool kit

Clear plastic adhesive pebbles

Rub-on transfers

Turquoise acrylic paint (in two shades of turquoise)

Textured paste

Foam roller

Circle cutters and blades

Photo tabs

Palette or old plate

1. Squeeze some acrylic colour into textured paste on a palette or old plate. This paste contains tiny clear beads which adds to the watery theme.

2. Mix the colour and the textured paste using a foam roller.

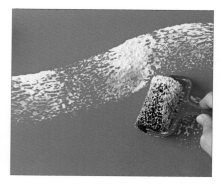

3. Roll the textured paint mix across your page in a loose, wave-like movement. Wash out your roller straight after use.

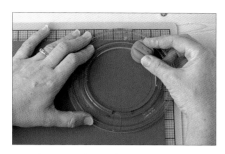

4. Place teal cardstock on a cutting mat and position a circle cutter on top. Pull the blade around the circle, holding it against the plastic. Use the same technique to cut more circles from card or vellum and to cut out details from your photographs. Vary the size of circle cutter that you use.

5. To create a 3D sticker, peel the backing off a clear plastic adhesive pebble and stick it on to the front of a photograph off-cut. Trim around it. Make several 3D stickers in this way to glue on to your page.

6. Use rub-on transfers to add text to your card circles and then attach the circles to your page with eyelets, using the eyelet tool kit.

I attached the photographs and vellum with photo tabs. Since tabs show through vellum, I slipped the vellum under the photographs so that they were hidden. The plastic pebbles can be strategically positioned to hold down vellum, too. I created the word 'Pool' for the title using the technique described on page 40. Note that the photographs cross over the break between the two pages so that the whole layout is unified.

Mosaics

Mosaics are simple and satifisfying to make and they create something entirely new from well-loved photographs. It is best to start off with squares and rectangles but once you feel inspired you can use all manner of shapes.

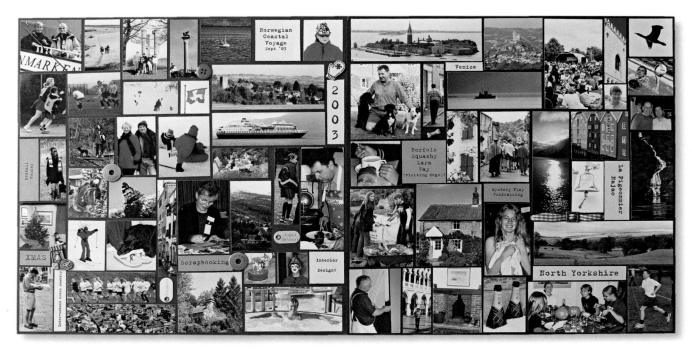

2003

This is a random selection of 'left over' photos from 2003. I started from the outside of the layout and worked inwards, filling any gaps with text and embellishments. It was easy work – just one evening in front of the television!

Using templates to start a mosaic

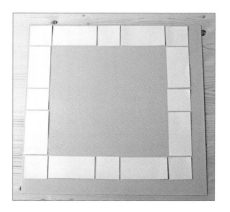

Before you start to cut up your photographs, it is a good idea to work out exactly how many squares and rectangles you need for your mosaic. The simplest way to do this is to cut out squares and rectangles from scrap paper and experiment with positioning them on the page. Then use your scrap paper arrangement as a guide as you cut and position your photographs.

Kephalonia

This is a simple but beautiful mosaic that allows the pictures to speak for themselves. I cut the two main photographs into six equally-sized squares and used a small square craft punch to make squares for the border. You can adapt this design to any theme.

1. Use a square punch to cut out as many squares of card and photograph as you need to create a border around the edge of your card. As you arrange the squares, try to give a random feel to the pattern, varying light and dark squares and spreading out coloured squares. Repositionable tape will allow you to adjust and refine the arrangement as you work and help you to create an even mosaic.

2. Using a trimmer, slice your main photograph into six equal parts. Repeat with another favourite photograph. Reassemble the pictures within the border and finally add a line of mosaic squares across the middle.

The finished page. I typed the title on the background cardstock using an A3 printer. I assembled the mosaic as shown, trimmed the cardstock after assembly and double-mounted it before attaching the whole picture to the background using photo tabs. Embellishments formed the finishing touch.

Index

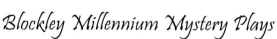

Blockley Millennium Mystery Plays

I have used the silhouetting technique shown on page 36. This is a good way of fitting a lot of pictures of people on a page – especially if they are from an event where the background is distracting. Placing the text amongst the people helps to avoid some of the difficulties with silhouetting described in the tip on page 37.

Equipment Used

Food Processor / Double Bladed Chopper: used for chopping and mincing ingredients i.e. garlic, onions and meat. Also use to chop vegetables for stir fries and bread for breadcrumbs etc. If using a mini chopper remember not to overload and prepare in smaller batches. Take care when handling the blades as they are extremely sharp!

Top Tip: Clean once food has been removed by pouring a little warm soapy water into the processor and pulse a few times.

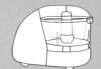

Blender / Stick Blender / Food Mixer: May be used for preparing soups, mayonnaise and smoothies. Also great for making up batters and cake mixes (may be done in a food mixer - stated when relevant.)
A blender / stick blender is great at rescuing lumpy sauces. Simply put them into the blender / bowl with stick blender and pulse a few times for a lump free sauce. For a lovely gloss to your sauces add a 1cm cube of cold butter.

Some blenders / stick blenders are considerably more powerful and versatile than others. They can chop & grind, make cakes & smoothies. Some blenders even make & heat soups. *Use your discretion in the recipes featured as to which piece of equipment to use.*

Top Tip: Clean once food has been removed by pouring a little warm soapy water into the plastic beaker, pulse a few times and rinse.

Multi-Mill or Wet & Dry Mill: May be used for grinding spices, chopping herbs, cheeses, chocolate coffee beans, turning sugar into the consistency of icing sugar, making effused oils, coulis, breadcrumbs, smoothies, chopping garlic, parmesan, etc.

Do not use liquid in a dry mill. In this book I've used a mill compatible with liquids.

Top Tip: Clean once food has been removed by pouring a little warm soapy water into the mill and pulse a few times. Do not do this in a dry only mill. Always follow the manufacturers instructions.

For whisking we may use a range of equipment including:

A Stick Blender with a flat disk interchange or a balloon whisk attachment.
A Food Mixer with a balloon whisk.
An Electric Hand Mixer.

Use to aerate double cream, whipping cream and whisking egg whites for meringues. You may also whisk **virtually fat free ice cold** skimmed milk to achieve the consistency of cream. Please note however, that this will only hold for a short time. Great over fresh fruit as a topping or for speciality coffee. Looks great without adding calorie laden cream.

Contents / Index

Top Tip!...Basil oil makes a great dressing over salad or pasta.

Basil Oil Scallops

Ingredients   **Serves 4**

2 tbsp olive oil
20 basil leaves
Pinch salt & pepper
Pinch sugar
12 scallops
12 slices streaky bacon
1 tbsp thick balsamic glaze
2 handfuls baby spinach

Method

1. Place the basil, oil, sugar, salt and pepper in the wet / dry mill or multi-mill, chop and blend until fine a consistency achieved.
2. Divide the washed baby spinach onto four serving plates.
3. Fry the bacon in a pan for 5 minutes, add the scallops and cook until slightly browned on each side.
4. Display the scallops and bacon around the baby spinach and drizzle the basil dressing and balsamic glaze around the plate and serve.

Top Tip!...Tastes great in a potato salad or with grilled chicken.

Caesar Salad Dressing

Ingredients   **Serves 3 - 4**

Dressing
50g parmesan cheese
2 tbsp mayonnaise
50ml single cream
20ml white vinegar
1 clove garlic (peeled)
3 tbsp olive oil
Pinch salt & pepper
10g anchovies (optional)
¼ tsp English mustard
1 tsp lemon juice
Salad
25g croutons
1 Romaine lettuce
25g parmesan cheese shavings

Method

1. In the multi-mill / wet & dry mill chop the parmesan to a breadcrumb consistency, then add the mayonnaise, cream, vinegar, garlic, anchovies, olive oil, mustard, lemon juice, salt and pepper and mix.
2. Wash and dry and tear the lettuce into pieces, serve in a bowl drizzled with the Caesar dressing, sprinkle with parmesan cheese shavings and croutons.

Chinese Dumplings

Ingredients   **Serves 4**

Dough mix
200g plain flour
50g corn flour
125ml water
½ tsp salt

Filling
250g pork (cubed)
1 clove garlic (peeled)
2 tsp sweet chilli sauce
1 cm cube ginger (peeled)
½ tbsp sesame seed oil
1 tbsp soy sauce
½ tsp sugar
1 egg yolk
1 tsp rice vinegar
1 onion (peeled & quartered)
2 tbsp corn flour
Oil for frying or Water for steaming.

Method

1. Finely chop the ginger and garlic in the food processor / double bladed chopper bowl.
2. Add the onion and chop.
3. Add pork, sesame oil, soy sauce, sugar, egg yolk, vinegar, corn flour, season, chop to a pulp and set aside.
4. To make dough place the flour, corn flour, salt and 80ml of water in to food processor and blend.
5. Add 30ml of water and blend to a breadcrumb consistency.
6. Add the last 15ml of water then mould together into a dough.
7. Roll into 15 separate balls. Roll each ball flat and fill with a teaspoon of meat mixture.
8. Wet edges with water, fold up and seal them together.
9. Fry in hot oil until golden brown and thoroughly cooked, or steam for 15 - 20 minutes.

Mix plum & hoisin sauces to make accompanying dip.

Top Tip!...Fry some chicken with garlic and butter and mix with the mushroom soup to make a sauce.

Mushroom Soup

Ingredients

Serves 3-4

250g button mushrooms (washed)
½ onion (peeled & quartered)
1 clove garlic (peeled)
15g butter
1 dsp olive oil
1 tbsp flour
300ml milk
1 Vegetable or chicken stock cube
  mixed with 100ml warm water.
2 tbsp sweet sherry
Pinch salt & pepper
50ml double cream

Method

1. Put the garlic in the food processor / double bladed chopper bowl and finely chop.
2. Add the onion and finely chop.
3. Fry the onions, garlic, butter, olive oil, salt and pepper for 5 minutes.
4. Roughly chop the mushrooms in the food processor or double bladed chopper bowl (you may have to divide the mushrooms into two lots depending on the size of your processor bowl).
5. Add the mushrooms to the onions and continue to fry for 8 minutes.
6. Mix in the flour and cook for 2 minutes stirring continuously.
7. Slowly add the stock and sherry, stirring frequently.
8. Slowly add the milk and cream cook for 5 minutes stirring constantly.

Serve with crusty bread or croutons.

Top Tip!... You can use ham or pancetta instead of bacon.

Pea & Bacon Soup

Ingredients   **Serves 4**

2 bacon rashers
400g frozen peas
300ml chicken stock
½ onion (peeled & quartered)
1 clove garlic (peeled)
2 medium potatoes (peeled)
300ml whole milk
1 tbsp olive oil
15g butter
¼ tsp mixed herbs
Pinch salt and pepper
Pinch sugar
50ml cream

Method

1. Put onion and garlic in the food processor / double bladed chopper bowl and chop. Add the bacon and chop.
2. Add the mixture to a pan with the butter and oil, fry for 5 minutes.
3. Add potatoes, peas, stock, sugar, herbs, salt & pepper to the pan and boil for 10 minutes, stir occasionally.
4. Add the milk, bring to the boil and simmer for 10 minutes.
5. Use the stick blender or place in the blender and blend until the desired consistency.

Serve with a crusty bread roll and a drizzle of cream.

Top Tip!... This also works great as a light batter for fish.

Tempura Batter

Ingredients

Serves 4

Batter
100g corn flour
150g self-raising flour
450ml soda water
¼ tsp garlic salt
Pinch sugar
¼ tsp turmeric
Groundnut oil for frying

Selection of vegetables & prawns
Carrot (peeled)
Red pepper
Broccoli
Sugar snap peas
Raw prawns

Dipping Sauce
3 tbsp soy sauce mixed with 2 tbsp
   of sweet chilli sauce
3 tbsp mirin (sweet rice vinegar)
¼ carrot (peeled)
1 spring onion

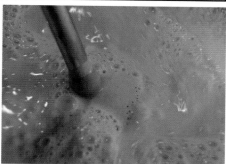

Method

1. Blend the corn flour, self-raising flour, soda water, garlic salt, sugar and turmeric using the stick blender / blender and or food mixer with balloon whisk attachment, set aside.
2. For the dipping sauce chop the carrot in the processor or double bladed chopper bowl.
3. Chop the spring onion, put into a bowl with soy sauce mixture, mirin and combine.
4. Cut the vegetables in to chunks.
5. Individually coat the vegetable chunks and prawns with the batter and fry in the hot ground nut oil until golden brown and cooked.

17

Top Tip!...Add 50g of chopped chorizo to the onions & garlic, to add a spanish twist. This also works great as a base for tomato dishes.

Tomato Soup

Ingredients   **Serves 4**

½ onion (peeled)
1 clove garlic (peeled)
1 tbsp olive oil
2 tins chopped tomatoes
1 vegetable or chicken stock
  cube mixed with 250ml boiling
  water.
2 tbsp tomato puree
Pinch salt & pepper
½ tsp sugar
Pinch dried mixed herbs
1 dsp balsamic glaze

Method

1. Place the garlic in the food processor or double bladed chopper bowl and finely chop. Add the onion and finely chop.
2. Fry the onions, garlic, olive oil, salt and pepper in a pan for 5 minutes.
3. Add the tomato puree and sugar and cook for 3 minutes.
4. Add the mixed herbs and balsamic glaze and stir, add the stock, chopped tomatoes and cook for 5 minutes.
5. Blend with the stick blender / blender and serve.

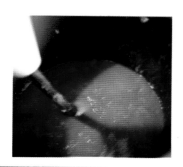

Serve with a crusty bread roll.

Top Tip!...You can use cooked chicken instead of tuna.

Tuna Filling

Ingredients

Serves 2

1 tin tuna (185g)
1 tbsp mayonnaise
½ tbsp ketchup
2 spring onions
Pinch garlic salt
1 carrot (peeled)
crusty breads / rolls

Method

1. Place the carrot in the food processor or double bladed chopper bowl and finely chop.
2. Add the spring onions and roughly chop.
3. Add the tuna, mayonnaise, ketchup, garlic salt and lightly chop together.

Serve in a crusty roll with a green salad or jacket potato.

Top Tip!... If you like it spicy add 1 tsp of paprika when you cook the onions. Also tastes delicious with grilled sausages!

Aubergine Parmigiana

Ingredients   **Serves 4**

2 aubergines (stalk removed,
  sliced)
4 tbsp olive oil
1 onion (peeled & quartered)
3 cloves garlic (peeled)
2 400g tins chopped tomatoes
4 tbsp tomato sauce
1 tsp dried mixed herbs
Pinch salt & pepper
125g parmesan (cubed)
1 handful oregano (optional)

Method

1. Chop the onion in the food processor or double bladed chopper bowl and set aside
2. Put 3 ½ tbsp olive oil in a hot pan, brown and soften the aubergine. Place in a bowl.
3. In the same frying pan fry, the onions for three minutes. Add the garlic and ½ tbsp of olive oil, fry for a further minute, then add the tomato sauce, mixed herbs, chopped tomatoes. Season with salt and pepper. Turn off heat.
4. In the food processor/double bladed chopper chop the parmesan to a breadcrumb consistency.
5. Layer the aubergine in an oven proof dish. Cover with the sauce and a dusting of parmesan. Repeat this process. Place in a hot oven at 200°c for 20 to 30 minutes until piping hot and starting to brown .

Top Tip!... Use prawns, thinly sliced pork or beef instead of chicken.

Chinese Stir Fry Chicken

Ingredients

Serves 2

1 clove garlic (peeled)
1 cm cube ginger (peeled)
1 onion (peeled & quartered)
1 tbsp sesame seed oil
1 tbsp soy sauce
½ tsp brown sugar
1 chicken or vegetable stock
   cube mixed with 100ml boiling
   water.
1 tbsp rice or wine vinegar
Pinch salt & pepper
2 chicken breasts
1 handful sugar snap peas
1 carrot (peeled)
1 red pepper
1 handful bean sprouts

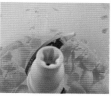

Method

1. Separately chop the pepper, carrot and onion in the food processor or double bladed chopper bowl and set aside.
2. Chop the garlic and ginger and set aside.
3. Slice the chicken into strips and fry in the sesame seed oil for 2 minutes stirring continuously.
4. Add the ginger and garlic, fry for 1 minute.
5. Add onion, fry for 1 minute.
6. Add the carrot and pepper, fry for 1 minute.
7. Add sugar snap peas and bean sprouts, fry for 1 minute.
8. Add rice vinegar, soy sauce, brown sugar and stock and cook for 5 minutes or until the chicken is thoroughly cooked.

**Top Tip!... You can use chicken or lamb instead
of sirloin steak.**

Chorizo & Refried Bean Wraps

Ingredients   **Serves 4**
½ onion (peeled & quartered)
1 400g tin mixed beans
 (in tomato sauce)
50g chorizo
¼ jalapeño pepper (add more if you like it spicy)
Pinch salt & pepper
8 flour tortilla wraps
1 sirloin steak (cut into strips)
Pinch coarse black pepper
100g chilli cheese or cheddar
 cheese

Method

1. Separately chop the cheese, chorizo and mixed beans using the food processor or double bladed chopper bowl and set aside.
2. Chop the onions and jalapeño pepper in the food processor or double bladed chopper bowl and set aside.
3. Fry the steak and black pepper in a hot pan for 5 minutes until brown and place in a separate bowl.
4. Using the same pan, fry the onions and chorizo until golden brown, season and add the beans. Fry for 3 - 4 minutes or until thoroughly heated.
5. To serve, place the tortilla on a plate and spread some of the bean mix over the surface. Add the beef and cheese before wrapping the tortilla.

Can be served with sour cream and guacamole.

Top Tip!... You can also use the red pepper crust as a stuffing for oily fish such as mackerel, trout or salmon.

Hake with a Red Pepper Crust Main

Ingredients   **Serves 4**

4 fillet portions of hake or any white fish

Red pepper crust
1 peeled roasted red pepper
1 tbsp olive oil
1 tbsp parsley
1 tbsp lemon juice
1 slice granary bread
1 tbsp tartar sauce
pinch salt & pepper

Method

1. Put the parsley and bread in to food processor or double bladed chopper bowl and chop to a crumb consistency.
2. Mix in and chop the lemon juice, tartar sauce, red pepper and olive oil.
3. Spread the mixture over the fish fillets and place in an oven proof dish.
4. Oven cook at 200°c for 20 -25 minutes until golden.

Serve with new potatoes, asparagus and broccoli.

29

Top Tip!... Turn this dish into chicken tikka masala by adding fried onions, coconut milk and a tin of condensed tomato soup. Garnish with ground almonds.

Hot Tandoori Paste

Ingredients   **Makes 6**
1 clove of garlic (peeled)
2 cm cube fresh ginger (peeled)
1 red chilli (stalk removed)
70ml vegetable oil
1 tsp salt
2 tsp flour
2 tbsp paprika
1 tbsp cumin seeds
1 tbsp garam masala
2 tsp lemon juice
¼ tsp white pepper
2 tbsp mango chutney
Tandoori Chicken
6 chicken thighs
2 tbsp natural yoghurt

Method
1. Finely chop the garlic, ginger and chilli in the food processor / double bladed chopper bowl.
2. Add the vegetable oil, salt, flour, paprika, cumin seeds, garam masala, lemon juice, white pepper and mango chutney. Blend to a paste and put into a bowl.
3. For Tandoori Chicken mix the paste with the yoghurt and coat the chicken thighs.
4. Place in an oven proof dish and bake at 200°c for 25 - 35 minutes until cooked.

The paste will last for up to two weeks in the fridge in a sealed container.

Top Tip!..You can use this herb crust on
individual lamb chops or lamb steaks.

Lamb with a Fresh Herb Crust

Ingredients   **Serves 2**

Herb crust
4 sprigs parsley
4 leaves sage
2 sprigs thyme (picked)
1 sprig rosemary (picked)
1 slice granary bread
2 tbsp olive oil

1 Rack of lamb
2 tbsp Honey
¼ tsp Mustard

Method

1. Chop the granary bread, parsley, sage, thyme and rosemary in the food processor / double bladed chopper bowl /multi-mill.
2. Mix the honey and mustard together, coat the rack of lamb and then roll in the crumb mixture.
3. Pour the oil onto a baking tray and place the lamb on the tray.
4. Bake in a preheated oven at 200°c for 25 - 45 minutes depending on the size of the rack of lamb and how well you like it cooked.

Top Tip!...For a peanut dip or peanut butter place salted peanuts into the grinder with some vegetable oil and grind to the preferred consistency.

Peanut Coated Pork Balls

Ingredients   **Makes 9-10**
250g diced pork
1 egg yolk
2 tbsp flour
1 clove garlic (peeled)
1 tsp cumin powder
1 tbsp sweet chilli sauce
Pinch salt & pepper
75g salted peanuts

Method

1. Finely chop the garlic in the food processor / double bladed chopper bowl.
2. Add the pork and chop to a fine mince.
3. Add the egg, cumin, flour, sweet chilli, salt and pepper and mix.
4. Roll into 9 or 10 balls of similar size.
5. Roughly chop the nuts in the food processor / double bladed chopper bowl.
6. Pour the nuts onto a plate and roll the balls in the nuts until coated.
7. Bake in the oven at 200°c for 20 - 25 minutes.

Top Tip!... Use roasted red pepper instead of basil for a red pepper pesto.

Pesto

Ingredients

Serves 4

Pesto
2 large hand fulls of basil leaves
4 tbsp olive oil
50g parmesan cheese
50g pine nuts
2 cloves of garlic (peeled)
Pinch salt & pepper

Method

1. Chop the garlic and parmesan in a food processor / double bladed chopper bowl.
2. Add the pine nuts, salt and pepper and chop.
3. Add the basil leaves and oil. Chop to desired consistency.

Serving suggestions:
Mix with cooked pasta and poached chicken.
Drizzle over sliced mozzarella and tomatoes.
Pour over grilled salmon and asparagus.

Top Tip!...Great as a topping for jacket potatoes, white fish or cauliflower.

Main

Quick Cheese Sauce for Macaroni

Ingredients   **Serves 4**

500ml milk
10g butter
1 tbsp heaped cornflour mixed
  with a little water
1 vegetable or chicken stock cube
  mixed with 100ml warm water.
Pinch of garlic salt
60g extra mature cheddar
1 onion (peeled & quartered)
1 garlic clove (peeled)
3 rashers streaky bacon (sliced)
125g broccoli florets
350g macaroni pasta
Pinch salt & pepper

Method

1. Boil the macaroni pasta for 13 minutes; 3 minutes before the end add the broccoli then drain and set aside.
2. Place the garlic in the food processor / double bladed chopper until finely chopped.
3. Add the onion and continue until finely chopped.
4. Slice the bacon and place in the pan with the onion, garlic, butter, salt and pepper and fry for 8 minutes then set aside.
5. Bring the milk, garlic salt and stock to the boil. In a separate pan slowly pour in the cornflour whilst blending the mixture with a stick blender to make the sauce.
6. Add the onions, garlic mix and bacon, into the sauce.
7. Add half the cheese and stir the mixture.
8. Place pasta and broccoli in an oven proof dish. Pour over cheese sauce and sprinkle with the remaining cheese.
9. Place in the oven at 250°c for 10 minutes or until golden brown and serve.

39

Top Tip!...Add another tsp of paprika and ½ tsp of chilli powder to the coating mix, for spicy fried chicken.

Southern Fried Chicken

Ingredients   **Makes 6**

6 chicken thighs
Oil for frying
Marinade
150ml sour cream
½ tsp celery salt
¼ tsp mild chilli powder
¼ tsp white pepper
¼ tsp cinnamon
¼ tsp garlic salt
Coating Mix
3 tbsp plain flour
1 slice of granary bread
¼ tsp cinnamon
¼ tsp paprika
¼ tsp celery salt
¼ tsp garlic salt
¼ tsp dried mixed herbs
¼ tsp dried sage

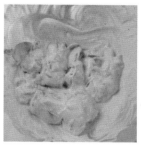

Method

1. In a bowl mix together the sour cream, celery salt, chilli powder, white pepper, cinnamon and garlic salt in a bowl. Add in the chicken thighs and marinade for 10 minutes.
2. To make the coating place the bread, flour, cinnamon, paprika, celery salt, garlic salt, mixed herbs and sage in the food processor / double bladed chopper bowl and chop to a crumb consistency.
3. Coat the chicken in the coating mix.
4. Fry in a hot pan with the oil for 5 minutes on each side or until cooked and golden brown.

Top Tip!...You can also stuff pork chops,
bell peppers or flat mushrooms.

Stuffed Chicken Thighs

Ingredients   **Makes 6**

6 chicken thighs
6 strips streaky bacon
Stuffing Mix
½ onion (peeled & quartered)
2 slices granary bread
200g sausage meat
Salt & pepper
1 egg
25g parsley (12g if using dried)
25g sage (12g if using dried)
Filling Variations
50g apple (peeled & cubed)
or 50g cranberry or redcurrant
or 50g peaches
or 25g walnuts
or 50g sweet chilli sauce
or lemon & dill (½ lemon zest &
juice with 25g chopped dill for
fish)

Method

1. Finely chop the onion together with your chosen filling in the food processor or double bladed chopper bowl and set aside.
2. Finely chop the bread, parsley and sage in the food processor / double bladed chopper bowl and set aside.
3. In a bowl mix the onion, and chosen filling together with the herb breadcrumbs, sausage meat, egg and salt and pepper.
4. Put the stuffing into your chicken and wrap with bacon or in chosen meat, vegetable or fish.
5. Bake in the oven at 180°c for 30 – 40 minutes until cooked.

Top Tip!... Mix with roasted vegetables for a tasty salad.

Tabouli

Ingredients **Serves 4**

1 medium onion
  (peeled & quartered)
1 clove garlic (peeled)
25g parsley
2 tomatoes
50g dried bulgur wheat (cook as
per instructions on packet)
1 tbsp olive oil
½ squeezed lemon
5 mint leaves
Pinch of salt & pepper

Method

1. Finely chop the garlic in the food
   processor / double bladed chopper bowl.
   Add the onion and finely chop. Pour into
   a large bowl and set aside.
2. Finely chop the parsley and mint in the
   food processor / double bladed chopper
   bowl. Add to the onions and garlic to the
   large bowl and set aside.
3. Roughly chop the tomato in the food
   processor / double bladed chopper bowl.
   Add to the other ingredients and set
   aside.
4. Add the cooked bulgur wheat, olive oil,
   lemon juice, salt and pepper to the rest
   of the ingredients in the large bowl and
   mix together.

Serve with grilled chicken in a pita bread.

45

Top Tip!...You can use chicken or lamb instead
of the turkey.

Turkey Burgers

Ingredients   **Makes 6**
500g turkey meat (cubed)
¼ onion (peeled & quartered)
2 slices granary bread
5 sprigs parsley
1 garlic clove (peeled)
1 tsp mixed herbs
2 tbsp plain flour
1 small egg
1 tbsp cranberry sauce
Oil for cooking

Method

1. Finely chop the garlic in the processor / double bladed chopper bowl. Add the onion and bread, finely chop and set aside in a large bowl.
2. Blend meat, parsley, herbs, egg, flour and cranberry sauce in processor / double bladed chopper bowl. Add the meat mixture, bread, garlic and onions in the large bowl.

3. Mix together and shape into burgers. Cook burgers with a little oil on a shallow tray in oven at 200°c for 20 -25 minutes.

Serve in crusty bread with a tomato and onion salad.

Top Tip!... Add cocktail sausages to method 4. for toad in the hole.

Yorkshire Puddings with Onions & Bacon

Ingredients   **Makes 6**

250 ml milk
100ml water
2 eggs
175g plain flour
Pinch salt
1 tbsp vegetable oil or lard
½ onion (peeled)
3 rashers streaky bacon (optional)

Method

1. Finely chop the onion in the food processor / double bladed chopper bowl.
2. Place the milk, water, eggs, salt and flour in a food mixer with a balloon whisk or use a bowl and stick blender and blend. Mix to a smooth batter.
3. Chop the bacon and add with the onion to the batter. Stir with a spoon.
4. Pour the oil into 5 muffin moulds and heat in a preheated oven at 230°c for 5 minutes. (You can use smaller moulds to make more Yorkshires if desired)
5. Once heated remove from the oven and pour the batter mix evenly into each mould.
6. Place back into the oven at 230°c for 25 - 35 minutes until cooked.

Top Tip!...You can use chopped apple instead of banana.

Banana Cake

Ingredients   **Serves 6**
150g self raising flour
150g butter (room temperature)
150g caster sugar
3 large eggs
2 soft bananas (peeled & sliced)
1 tsp vanilla essence
1 tsp soft butter

Method

1. Mix the flour, butter, sugar, eggs and vanilla essence either in a bowl using a stick blender or food mixer with a cake attachment.
2. Add the sliced banana to the mixture. Continue mixing until the banana resembles small chunks.
3. Grease a loaf tin 240mm x 100mm and pour in the cake mixture.
4. Bake at 200°c for 40 – 50 minutes.

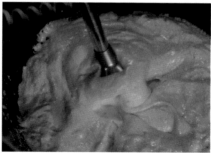

Serve with fresh banana and cream or ice cream.

Top Tip!... You can use a pre-bought flan base instead of a cookie base.

Chocolate Banoffee Pie

Ingredients   **Serves 6**

Base
200g chocolate chip cookies
50g butter (melted)
Topping
1 tin ready made caramel
   sweetened condensed milk (370g)
2 bananas (peeled & sliced)
½ pint double cream
1 chocolate flake

Method

1. Chop the chocolate chip cookies in the food processor / double bladed chopper bowl.
2. Add the melted butter and mix.
3. Spread the cookie mix around the base of a 5 inch round dish and flatten down.
4. Whip the cream in a food mixer with a balloon whisk or in a bowl with a stick blender.
5. Spread the caramel sweetened condensed milk over the top of the cookie base.
6. Slice the bananas and arrange on top.
7. Spoon the cream over the bananas.
8. Decorate with a broken chocolate flake.

53

Top Tip!...The frosting can be used as a
filling for a large chocolate cake.

Chocolate Cupcakes

Ingredients   **Makes 12 - 18**

Cupcake
150g butter
2 eggs
150g self raising flour
150g sugar
40ml whole milk
40g cocoa powder
½ tsp vanilla essence
12 cup cake cases

Frosting
500g icing sugar
170g unsalted butter (room temp)
80g cocoa powder
½ tsp vanilla essence
40ml whole milk
1 tsp gravy browning
100g chocolate chips (optional)
12 glacé cherries (optional)

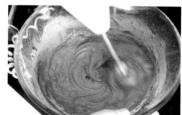

Method

1. Mix together butter, eggs, flour, sugar, cocoa powder, milk and vanilla essence in a bowl with stick blender or food mixer with a cake attachment.
2. Divide into 12 cupcake cases and place in a cupcake tin.
3. Bake in the oven at 170°c for 25 - 35 minutes. During baking time put the icing sugar, butter, cocoa, vanilla essence, milk & gravy browning in a bowl and mix together with a stick blender or food mixer with cake attachment.
4. When cooked remove the cupcakes from the oven and cool.
5. Pipe or spoon the frosting on top of each cupcake and decorate with glacé cherries or chocolate chips. (Store in sealed container).

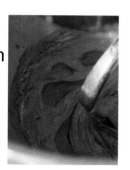
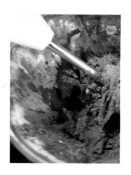

Top Tip!... The crumble topping can be made in advance and frozen for future use.

Crumble

Ingredients **Serves 4-6**

Crumble ingredients
75g butter
150g flour
75g brown sugar
75g granary bread

Filling:
500g of fruit. Sweeten to taste
        with sugar.

Filling Variations:
Apple & peach
or apple, berry & plum
or rhubarb & sultana

Method

1. Put the bread into the food processor / double bladed chopper bowl. Chop into breadcrumbs. Place into a large bowl.
2. Put the butter, flour & sugar into the food processor / double bladed chopper bowl. Chop to a breadcrumb consistency.
3. Add the flour mixture to the breadcrumbs and combine together to form the crumble.
4. Place the fruits in to an ovenproof dish. Sweeten to taste. Add the crumble mix as a topping.
5. Cook in a preheated oven at 180°c for 20 - 25 minutes or until golden brown.

Serve with ice cream, cream or custard.

Top Tip!...The cake makes a great base for trifle.

Lemon & Orange Drizzle Cake

Ingredients   **Serves 6**

150g self raising flour
75g castor sugar
75g dark brown sugar
150g butter (very soft / room
        temperature)
3 eggs
1 orange (zest & juice)
1 lemon (zest & ½ juice)
150g icing sugar

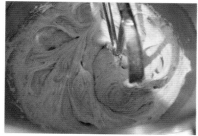

Method

1. Put the the butter, castor sugar, brown sugar, flour, eggs, ½ lemon zest, ½ orange zest and a tsp of orange & lemon juice in a bowl and mix with the stick blender or in a food mixer with the cake attachment.
2. Grease a 240x100mm loaf tin or silicon baking mold and pour in the mixture.
3. Bake at 170°c for 35 - 50 minutes until cooked.
4. Mix the remaining orange juice / zest and lemon juice / zest with the icing sugar.
5. Once the cake has cooled drizzle the zested icing sugar over the top of the cake.

Top Tip!...You can use milk instead of rice or oats and water. If a recipe requires rice flour use Method 1

Oat or Rice Milk Smoothies

Ingredients
Serves 2

Rice or Oat Milk
50g rice or oats
150ml water
1 tsp honey or sugar

Variations:
1 banana
½ mango
1 peach
25g blueberries
50g strawberries
25g raspberries

Method

1. Grind the rice or oats to a fine powder in a multi-mill / wet & dry mill or a very strong blender.
2. Add water and honey or sugar. Blend until milk colour.
3. Add one or more of the variations above and blend for a delicious smoothie.
4. Pour over ice ice and serve.

As a milk substitute use the rice / oat milk to tea / coffee.

Top Tip!...You can use other fruits such as apple
blueberries, sultanas and pineapple.

Peach & Raspberry Muffins

Dessert

Ingredients   **Makes 6**

75ml vegetable oil or melted butter
75ml milk
75g light brown castor sugar
1 egg
150g self raising flour
Pinch salt
1 peach (peeled & diced)
100g raspberries
½ tsp vanilla essence
6 muffin cases

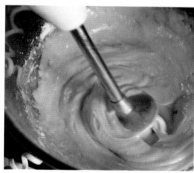

Method

1. Put the vegetable oil, milk, sugar, egg, flour, salt and vanilla essence in a bowl and mix using the stick blender / food mixer with cake attachment.
2. Carefully fold in the peaches and raspberries holding back 12 raspberries for decoration.
3. Divide into 6 muffin cases. Place in a muffin tin and bake in the oven at 170°c for 30 - 40 minutes. Cool and serve.

Top Tip!... Mix with whipped double cream to
        make a quick cheats berry bavarois.

Port Coulis

Ingredients   **Serves 2**
25ml port
100g castor sugar
100g mixed frozen berries

Method

1. Put castor sugar in the multi-mill or wet and dry mill.
   And process until very fine, like icing sugar.
2. Add the defrosted berries or fresh berries and the port.
   Mill until a fine consistency. Sieve to remove pips.
3. Place in a jug until ready to use.

Serve over ice cream, sorbet or around a dessert.

Appliance Guide

Important ! Please Read....

Always make sure any thing you put in your food processor is cut into a size that the machine can process.

Always follow manufacturers instructions. Always place the food in the correct bowl. Never leave your appliance unattended.

Always follow manufacturers cleaning instructions. Be very carefull when cleaning sharp blades.

All temperatures, times and instructions are given as a rough guide. Adjust accordingly, if needed, at time of cooking.

Always check that the food has been thoroughly cooked before consumption.

Mirin (sweet rice vinegar) As a substitite you can use 3 tbsp malt vinegar with ½ tbsp sugar.

Basmati rice is best served with Indian food as its quite sticky.

Easy cook rice is best for stir frys as it is less likely to stick together.

Some of the step by step photos are showing doing the same thing with different products, to show how different equipment can be used. Such as pages: 7, 9, 51, 55, 59, 61.

The soup recipes are for a hearty thick soup if you prefer thinner soups dilute with water, milk or stock.

All recipes and instructions are as a guide only. Always ensure they are compatible with your appliance. The manufacturers instructions should always take precedence.